The Wonderful Story of Jesus

Written by: David R. Collins

Illustrated by: Don Kueker
and Bill Hoyer

Concordia Publishing House
St. Louis

Copyright © 1980 by Concordia Publishing House
3558 South Jefferson Avenue, St. Louis, MO 63118

Library of Congress Cataloging in Publication Data

Collins, David R
    The wonderful story of Jesus.

    SUMMARY: Retells the life of Jesus from the angel's announcement
to Mary to Jesus' Ascension into heaven.
    1. Jesus Christ—Biography—Juvenile literature.
2. Christian biography—Palestine—Juvenile literature. [1. Jesus
Christ—Biography. 2. Bible stories—N.T.] I. Title.
BT302.C63   232.9′01   79-27585
ISBN 0-570-03490-6

*This book, the story of God's Son Jesus,
is dedicated to my own godson,
Ryan Richard Collins*

THE SAVIOR IS BORN

People were waiting.
They had been waiting for a long time.
They were waiting for the Savior
    God had promised them.
"He will come," said the old men.
"God will send Him," said the teachers.
"We will wait and pray," said the people.
And they did.

In a little town in Nazareth
    lived a young woman named Mary.
She was a happy girl, quiet and cheerful.
She carried water from the well.
She picked dates from the trees.
Like everyone else, she waited and prayed
    for the Savior to come.
Also in Nazareth there lived a man named Joseph.
He was a carpenter, hardworking and kind.
He made wood into chairs and tables.
He made wood into doors and wheels.
Like everyone else, he waited and prayed
    for the Savior to come.

One day Mary suddenly saw a bright light.
From the light came a voice.
"Mary, you are a special woman.
You are special to God."
Mary trembled.
Who was this speaking to her?
Could it be an angel?
What did his words mean?
Again the voice spoke.
"Do not be afraid, Mary.
God has chosen you to be the mother of His Son.
His Son shall be called Jesus.
He is the Savior people have been waiting for."
Mary thought about what the angel was saying.
She was to have a child—the Son of God!
Yet how could this be? she wondered.
She was not married.
"But how shall this happen?" Mary asked.
"It will happen through the power of God.
Do not be afraid.
God will guide you."
The words were kind.
The voice was gentle.
Mary felt safe.
"I shall be God's servant," she said.
"I will do anything He wishes."
The bright light disappeared.
Mary smiled.
She had a secret.
It was a wonderful secret.
For awhile Mary kept the secret to herself.
Soon she knew she must share her happy news.
She went to visit her cousin Elizabeth.

Luke 1:26-39

"I am to have a baby," Mary told Elizabeth.
"He will be the Son of God."
Elizabeth could not believe what she was hearing.
"Oh, Mary," she said, "You are truly blessed!
I have good news too.
An angel of the Lord came to my husband.
I am going to have a baby.
Think of it, in my old age I am at last
　　to have a son.
His name is to be John."
Mary hugged her cousin Elizabeth.
"God has blessed us both!" Mary exclaimed.
For three months Mary stayed with Elizabeth
Then she went back to Nazareth.

Luke 1:40-56

Joseph was waiting for her.
He was waiting to take her for his wife.
God had sent an angel to Joseph
    telling him the great plan.
Joseph gladly married Mary.
Spring became summer.
Then summer slipped into fall.
The first winds of winter stirred
    through the trees.
Matthew 1:18-25

One day Joseph took Mary's hand.
"We must go to the city of Bethlehem," he said.
"A count is being taken of all people.
Everyone must go to the city
    from which his family came.
Our family is of the house of David
    in Bethlehem."

Mary looked into her husband's eyes.
She knew he was worried.
The baby would soon be coming.
"We will go to Bethlehem," whispered Mary.
"The baby and I will be fine.
He will be born in the city of David
    as God's prophets foretold."
Together Mary and Joseph set out for Bethlehem.
She sat on a donkey, and he walked by her side.
Along dusty roads and across hillsides
    they traveled.
Finally, they reached Bethlehem.

The city of Bethlehem was crowded.
Travelers filled the streets and inns.
Everywhere Joseph and Mary went,
   the answer was the same.
"We have no room."
"This inn is filled."
"You cannot stay here."
Again Joseph asked, and again and again.
"No room," came the answer.
"No room in this inn."

Finally one innkeeper did not turn them away.
"My inn is all filled," he said.
"But my stable is near.
Stay there if you wish."
"Thank you," answered Joseph.
"You are good and kind."
The stable was warm in the cool winter night.
The straw was clean.
The animals were quiet.
"It is time," whispered Mary.
Joseph took his love's hand.
That night in the stable, baby Jesus was born.
A star cast a bright light in the sky.
Gently Mary wrapped the baby in swaddling clothes.
She put tiny Jesus in a manger of straw.
"The straw will keep Him warm," she said softly.

Suddenly men appeared at the stable entrance.
Mary and Joseph did not know the men.
"Who are you?" Joseph asked.
"We are shepherds," answered one man.
"We were watching our sheep
    when an angel appeared.
The angel told us our King had been born.
Our Savior had been born in Bethlehem."
A second man stepped forward.
"The angel said we would find the Babe
    in a manger.
It is all just as the angel said it would be."
A third shepherd smiled down at the baby Jesus.
"We have heard angels singing a wonderful song.
They sang, 'Glory to God in the highest.
Peace on earth among men of good will.'"
Mary knelt beside the manger.
Joseph stood beside her.
They looked down at the baby Jesus.
The newborn Savior slept peacefully.
            Luke 2:1-20

Later more visitors came to see Jesus.
One night some travelers came from far away.
They were teachers and Wise Men.
"We have followed a star all the way
        from our distant homes.
Could it be that it has brought us to the new king?
We have read the old books.
They have told us a new Savior would come."
"The star has led you well," said Joseph.
"Come see the baby Jesus," said Mary.
The Wise Men were happy.
They gave the newborn Savior gifts
        of gold, frankincense, and myrrh.
Mary and Joseph smiled.
They were glad God had shared His Son with them.

Very shortly after the visit of the Wise Men,
Joseph awoke from a disturbing dream.
God had sent an angel with a message:
"Take the child and His mother and go to Egypt.
King Herod wants to find Him and kill Him.
Stay in Egypt until I tell you
        it is safe to return."
Right away Joseph obeyed.
They escaped to Egypt.
King Herod in Jerusalem had met with the Wise Men
        and knew about the new king.
He had invited the Wise Men to return and tell him
        where the new king could be found
        so he could go to worship Him, he said.
The Wise Men went home another way
        and didn't return to tell King Herod.
Herod was angry.
He ordered that all boys under the age of two
        should be killed.
Herod was afraid that the newborn king
        would take over his earthly kingdom.

The weeks and months slipped by.
God sent a message to Joseph in another dream.
It was safe for them to return.
Joseph took Mary and Jesus back to Palestine.
And it was in the city of Nazareth
        that Jesus grew up.
All these things happened
        just the way the prophets said they would.
                Matthew 2:1-23

YOUNG JESUS

When Jesus was 12 years old,
Mary and Joseph told Him exciting news.
"We are going to the city of Jerusalem
to celebrate the Passover," said Joseph.
"We are going to see the great temple of God,"
said Mary.
Jesus was happy, because this time
He was going along.
He had heard people talk about
the great house of God
in the great city of Jerusalem.
Teachers were there.
They told wonderful stories
about God and His people.
Jesus could hardly wait to get to Jerusalem.

From Nazareth to Jerusalem was a long journey.
It was almost 100 miles.
"Please hurry," Jesus begged as they traveled.
"I want to visit God's great house."
The temple in Jerusalem was a fine place.
Jesus prayed.
He listened to the teachers
     tell stories about God.
Quickly the hours slipped away.
Soon it was time to go back to Nazareth.
Mary and Joseph left Jerusalem.
They had met other travelers
     who would be going back to Nazareth.
It would be a happier journey
     traveling with friends.
After traveling a full day, Mary turned to Joseph.
"Have you seen Jesus?" she asked.
"He must be with our friends," Joseph answered.
Together Mary and Joseph looked for Jesus.
They could not find Him anywhere.

Quickly Mary and Joseph returned to Jerusalem.
Up and down the streets they looked.
In and out of buildings they looked.
Where could Jesus be?
On the third day Mary and Joseph went to the temple.
There sat Jesus, surrounded by teachers.
But He was teaching them!
He was telling *them* stories about God.
"Jesus," His mother said.
"Your father and I have been looking for You.
We have been so worried.
Why have You done this to us?
We did not know where You were."
Jesus was surprised.
"Where were you looking for Me?
Did you not know I must be doing work
     for God, My Father?"

Mary and Joseph did not know what Jesus meant.
They took Him back to Nazareth.
He was obedient to His parents.
          Luke 2:41-51

Days became weeks.
Months became years.
The boy Jesus grew to manhood.
He became a carpenter like Joseph.
Jesus was strong and wise.

As Jesus grew older, He heard stories
    about His cousin John.
John was the son of Elizabeth
    and just about the same age as Jesus.
John had given his life to God.
He served God every day.
He prayed with men, women, and children.
He baptized them in water.
He told them to be sorry for their sins.
    Matthew 3:1-12, Mark 1:1-8,
    Luke 2:52—3:18, John 3:19-31

JESUS THE TEACHER

*J*esus went to the Jordan River.
He knew John would be baptizing people there.
"Will you baptize Me?" asked Jesus.
John knew Jesus was the Son of God.
"You are the Lord, our Savior," said John.
"I should ask You to baptize me."
Jesus smiled.
"John, you are a good and holy man.
It is God's wish that you baptize Me."
John would do anything for God.
He was happy to baptize Jesus.
Suddenly the sky seemed to break open.
The Holy Spirit in the form
     of a beautiful white bird
     flew down from above.
It was a dove, the bird of peace and love.
From the sky came a voice.
"This is My beloved Son," said the voice.
"I am very pleased with Him."
     Matthew 3:13-17, Mark 1:9-11,
     Luke 3:21-22, John 3:32-34

Jesus was ready to begin His work here on earth.
He needed time to pray and talk with God,
    His Father.
Immediately after His baptism,
    Jesus went out into the wilderness.
Alone, Jesus went into a big, quiet desert,
    where there were only wild beasts,
        snakes and insects.
All day long Jesus talked to God.
All night long Jesus talked to God.
For 40 days Jesus talked to God.
He ate nothing.
Jesus became very hungry.

Suddenly Jesus heard a voice in the desert.
"Look all around You," the voice said.
"Look at the stones everywhere.
Turn them into bread and eat them.
Then You will not be hungry."
Jesus knew He could do what the voice said.
But whose voice was this?
It was not the wonderful voice of God.
God would not tempt Jesus
    to use His power for Himself.
This was an evil voice.
It had to be the devil.
"The Bible says: 'A person needs more
    than food for his body,'" Jesus answered.
"A person needs the love of God
    to feed his mind and soul."

The devil would not leave Jesus alone.
The devil used his power to take Jesus
    to a tall temple.
"If You are the Son of God, throw Yourself down."
The devil smiled an ugly smile.
"Surely the angels of God will save You."
Jesus shook His head.
"The Bible says: 'You should not
    tempt the Lord,'" He replied.

Still the devil would not leave.
He had a final plan.
With his power, he took Jesus to a great mountain.
"From here you can see all the kingdoms
    of the world."
The devil smiled an ugly smile.
"These kingdoms have fine jewels.
These kingdoms have grand clothes.
These kingdoms have rich food and treasures.
All these can be Yours.
All You must do is fall on Your knees.
Pray to me and promise to serve me."
Once more Jesus shook His head.
"The Bible says: 'You should worship
    no one but God,'" He stated.
"God alone is the One I serve.
Go away. Leave me, now!"

The devil knew he had lost.
The power of God was too strong.
Quickly the devil disappeared.
Angels came and brought Jesus food.
He knew He had not been alone in the desert.
God had been with Him.
Jesus was ready to do God's work.
    Matthew 4:1-11, Mark 1:12-13, Luke 4:1-13

If only everyone could know about God!
God's love gives hope.
God's love gives strength.
God's love gives comfort.
Jesus began to tell everyone
    about the love of God.
Everywhere Jesus went, people listened to Him.
To cities and towns Jesus traveled.
To the mountains and into the valleys.
Across the plains and the fields.
Some people welcomed Jesus; others feared Him.
Some didn't know who He was,
    but wanted to know more about Him.
"Tell us more about God," they begged.
"Please stay with us longer."

"God, I need help to carry Your message,"
    Jesus prayed.
"Please lead Me to those
    who would serve You best."
God was listening to Jesus' prayers.
God always listens to those who want His help.
God helped Jesus find good workers.
Jesus found His first two helpers in a boat
    by the Sea of Galilee.
They were fishing.
"Come follow Me," said Jesus.
"I will make you fishers of men."
Simon Peter and Andrew became
    the first two helpers of Jesus.
Jesus walked farther along the seashore.
He saw two brothers mending their fishing nets.
"Come with Me," said Jesus.
"I will help you mend the souls of people."
James and John, the sons of Zebedee,
    became the next helpers of Jesus.
        Matthew 4:17-22, Mark 1:14-20, Luke 6:12

Later on Jesus came to a place
    where tax money was collected.
"Come with Me," Jesus said
    to a man named Matthew (or Levi).
"I will help you collect people to love God."
Matthew got up and became a helper of Jesus.
    Matthew 9:9, Mark 2:14, Luke 5:27-28

Jesus had five helpers, then six, seven, and eight.
A man named Philip, then Thomas and Bartholomew.
Eight became nine, then ten and eleven.
Thaddeus, another Simon and another James
    joined them.
The last was named Judas, who later betrayed Him.
    Matthew 10:2-4, Mark 3:13-19, Luke 6:13-16

Jesus had selected his twelve helpers.
"You are My disciples," He told them.
"We will take the message of God's love
    everywhere."

Jesus' message was very clear:
"God loves all people, even those
    who have done many wrong things.
Those who follow Me should also love all people.
A wonderful world awaits those who believe in Me;
    it is the kingdom of heaven."

The people listened.
Jesus' words were so simple,
  but different from anything they had ever heard.
People came from far and near to hear Jesus teach.
When Jesus saw the large crowd gathered,
  He went up on a hill and taught them.
He told the people:
"Blessed are those who know their need of God,
  for the kingdom of heaven is theirs.
Blessed are those who mourn and are sorrowful,
  for they shall be comforted.
Blessed are those who are gentle,
  for they shall own the earth.
Blessed are those who hunger and thirst
  for righteousness, for they shall be satisfied.
Blessed are those who show mercy,
  for they shall be shown mercy.
Blessed are those whose hearts are pure,
  for they shall see God.
Blessed are those who try to keep peace,
  for they shall be called God's children.
Blessed are those who are made to suffer
  for doing what is right,
  for the kingdom of heaven belongs to them.
Blessed are those who are hated,
  mistreated, and falsely accused,
  because they believe in Me.
Be happy! Be very happy!
God will always listen.
  For your reward is great in heaven.
This is what happened to the prophets
  who came before Me."
    Matthew 5:1-12, Luke 6:35-36, 20-23

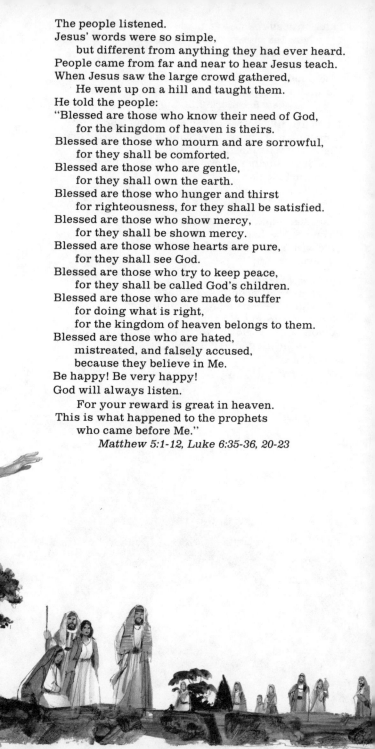

The disciples of Jesus listened to His words.
They watched Him share love with everyone He met.
He comforted people who were unhappy.
He healed the sick.
He taught people to pray.
"When you pray," said Jesus, "don't do it
    to show off or try to make yourself
    look good in public.
Pray in secret and quietly.
God will always listen.
Don't repeat words that have no meaning to you.
God, the Father, knows your needs
    even before you ask Him.
Pray like this:
Our Father who art in heaven, hallowed be Thy name.
    (God is our Father—a provider and protector.
    The name of God should be holy and respected
    above all things.)
Thy kingdom come.
Thy will be done on earth as it is in heaven.
    (Ask that God's rule will overcome
    all opposition.)
Give us this day our daily bread.
    (Ask God humbly for all your needs.)
And forgive us our debts, as we forgive our debtors.
    (Ask God to forgive your sins, and you forgive
    those who have sinned against you.)
And lead us not into temptation
    but deliver us from evil.
    (Ask God to protect you
    from the influences of evil.)
For Thine is the kingdom
    and the power and the glory forever."
    (God is Ruler and King with all the power
    to rule forever both in heaven and on earth.)
        Matthew 6:5-15, Luke 11:2-4

Sometimes parents brought their children to Jesus.
The disciples of Jesus scolded the parents.
"Jesus has many places to go.
He has many people to see.
He does not have time to talk with your children."
"Let the children come," Jesus told His disciples.
"They are children of God just as we are.
You must all become like these children
    if you are to enter the kingdom of heaven."
Jesus took the children into His arms
    and blessed them.
        Matthew 19:13-15, Mark 10:13-16, Luke 18:15-17

Jesus preached in the temple,
    and often Jesus talked with religious leaders
    and teachers.
They asked Him many questions.
Many of them didn't believe He was the Son of God.

One night a religious leader named Nicodemus
    came to where Jesus was staying.
"I believe you are sent from God," Nicodemus said.
He was afraid to say so in public.
Jesus smiled at the man.
"You must be born again," said Jesus.
"Before you can see the kingdom of heaven,
    you must be born again."
Nicodemus didn't understand.
"I am an old man.
How can I be born again?"
"Your body can't be born again,
    but your soul can," explained Jesus.
"God's Holy Spirit
    working through the water of Baptism,
    can make your soul fresh and new."
Nicodemus still didn't understand.
So Jesus explained more about how believing in Him
    brings people to heaven.
Then He said: "God loved the world so much
    that He sent His only Son.
Whoever believes in Him will not die,
    but will have life forever in heaven with God."
Nicodemus became a believer in Jesus.
        John 3:1-16

Jesus continued to comfort
    people who were unhappy.
Jesus continued to heal the lame and blind.
Jesus continued to teach God's wonderful message.
One day He called His disciples to Him.
He told them to go out and teach and heal
    "as you have seen Me do."
Tell the people about the kingdom of God.
"Take nothing with you," He told them.
The disciples went out and did
    as Jesus had told them.
      Matthew 10:1, 5-10, Mark 6:7-13, Luke 9:1-6

Jesus talked to people in their homes.
He spoke in the marketplaces.
He talked to travelers along the road.
"We are all children of God," Jesus taught.
"When we do wrong things, we must ask God
    for forgiveness.
If people do wrong things to us,
    we must forgive them.
We must treat our family and friends
    with kindness.
We must tell the truth.
We must not steal.
We must use good words.
This will make God happy."

A young lawyer approached Jesus.
"Tell us, Master, which of the ten commandments
    is the greatest."
Jesus answered:
"'Love God with all your heart, mind, and soul.'
This is the first and most important commandment.
The second commandment is like it:
'Love your neighbor as yourself.'
If you follow these two commandments,
    all the others will be fulfilled."
      Matthew 22:35-40, Luke 10:25-28

The people listened to Jesus.
They were amazed by what He said.
No other religious leader had ever spoken
    to them this way.
      Matthew 7:28-29, Mark 1:22

*J*esus often told special stories.
The stories were called parables.
Parables helped people
    to understand God's message.

"You must love your neighbor and be willing
    to help him in need," Jesus said.
"Who is my neighbor?" a man asked.
So Jesus told this parable.

A man was traveling along the road.
Suddenly, robbers jumped out
    from behind some rocks.
They took the man's money and beat him.
Quickly the robbers hurried away.
Soon another man, a priest, came traveling
    along the same road.
He saw the beaten man, but he did not stop.
He was too busy to help the stranger.
Another man, a Levite, came traveling
    along the the road.
He saw the beaten man, but he did not stop.
Why should I help a stranger? he thought.
Finally a man from Samaria traveled
    along the road.
The Samaritan jumped off his donkey
    when he saw the beaten man.
He cleaned the beaten man's wounds.
He took the man to an inn and cared for him
    and paid all the expenses.
"You must be a good neighbor
    like the good Samaritan,"
    Jesus told them.
(Samaritans were not liked
    by some people in Jesus' day.)
"All people are your neighbors."
The people listened.
Some of the people understood the story
    and tried to do what Jesus said.
Others refused to listen.
             Luke 20:25-37

"The kingdom of heaven is like a rich man
    who goes on a trip," said Jesus.
"Tell us the story," the people said.
"we want to hear it."
So Jesus told this parable.

A rich man had many servants.
To three servants he gave money.
"Take this money," he told one servant.
"And, here, take this money," he said to another.
"And here is some for you," he told a third.
The rich man went away.
One servant put the money he had been given
    into business and doubled it.
Another servant did the same.
The third servant buried his money
    and did nothing.
Later the rich man returned
    and asked about the money.
He was happy with the servants who had increased
    what he had given them.
"You have used the money wisely," he said.
"You both will be given more.
I will put you in charge
    of larger and better things."
But he was very unhappy with the servant
    who had buried his money.
"You wasted what I gave you.
You were lazy and unwise.
You are not worthy of the good things
    I have to offer."
        Matthew 25:14-30, Luke 19:12-24

The people listened.
Some people misunderstood and thought it was
    just a story.
"You must never think you are better than others,"
    said Jesus.
"Or you will be like the proud man in the temple."
"Tell us the story," the people begged.
"We want to hear it."
So Jesus told this parable.

Two men, a tax collector
    (tax collectors were often dishonest
    in those days) and a religious leader,
    went into the temple to pray.
The Pharisee stood tall and proud.
"I am a good man," he said before God and people.
"I obey Your rules.
I am kind and honest and true.
I'm not like other people, like that tax collector
    over there."
The Publican looked down.
He was too ashamed to look up.
"I sometimes break Your rules, God,"
    said the second man.
"I am a sinner.
But I will try to do better.
I do not deserve Your forgiveness.
But I pray for it anyway."
The two men left the temple.
God was not pleased with the proud man.
But the humble man had his sins forgiven.
                Luke 18:9-14

The people listened.
Some understood the message
        and promised to be more humble.
Others did not understand.
"God is happy when even one sinner repents,"
        said Jesus.
"Be willing to admit your mistakes.
Ask God for forgiveness like the foolish son."
"Tell us the story," people begged.
"We want to hear it."
So Jesus told the people this parable.

A rich man had two sons.
He planned to give his money to his sons someday.
But one son did not want to wait.
He asked his father for his share of the money.
The father gave the son his share.
Off the boy went, far away.
Soon he had spent every penny of the money.
He was a foolish boy, a prodigal son.
To stay alive, the boy went to work for a farmer.
He fed the pigs.
He ate their food.
He slept in the pigpen.
He was unhappy and he cried.
"Maybe my father will take me back,"
        said the boy.
"Maybe he will let me work as a servant."
The boy went home.

When his father saw his foolish son,
he hugged him.
"I am sorry," said the boy.
"I have broken God's rules and I have hurt you.
Forgive me."
The father called his servants.
"Tonight we will have a great feast," he said.
"My son has come back."

But the other son was confused and angry.
"I have stayed with you, father,
and worked for you."
The rich man smiled.
"Yes, and I love you for it.
But your brother was lost in the devil's world.
Now he has returned to the world of God
and to my house.
Let's be happy."

"God is like a loving father," said Jesus.
"He will forgive you if you ask Him and turn away
from sin.
Also, when someone comes back to God,
be sure to welcome that person back.
Don't be angry like the second son."
Luke 15:11-32

The people listened.
Some promised to ask God's forgiveness
    when they broke His rules.
Some promised to try harder not to break
    His rules.
But others didn't.
They didn't believe Jesus' teachings.
They wanted to go on living
    the way they always had.
"You must have strong faith in God
    and listen to My words," said Jesus.
"Or you will be like the man
    with a house built on sand."
"Tell us the story," people begged.
"We want to hear it."
So Jesus told them this parable.

A man built his house on rock.
Winds blew against his house.
Rains fell on it and floods came.
But the house stood strong and sturdy.
Another man built his house on sand.
Winds blew against the house.
Rains fell on it and floods came.
The house was soon ruined.
"Build your house of faith on rock," said Jesus.
Matthew 7:24-27

Jesus' teachings became well known.
What He taught was very different from anything
    the religious leaders had ever heard.
They were frightened and confused.
Some asked, "Is this *really* the Son of God?"
Others said, "Yes, I believe He is!"
John 7:40-43

*J*esus is God's Son.
He always was.
He is now.
He always will be.
While here on earth,
    Jesus did many wonderful things.
They were called miracles.

These miracles began when Jesus went
    to a wedding in the city of Cana.
His mother, Mary, was with Him.
After the wedding a party was held.
People at the party talked and laughed.
They ate and drank.
Jesus was glad to see His friends so happy.
Suddenly His mother came to Jesus.
"Our friends have no more wine.
They have shared with everyone
    who came to their party.
I wish we could help them."
"Send the servants to Me," Jesus said.
Quickly the servants came.
"Fill all the empty wine jars with water,"
    said Jesus.
The servants looked surprised.
But they did as Jesus told them.
"Now take your master a drink from the jars,"
    Jesus said.
Again the servants obeyed.
The master took a big drink.
"This is fine wine," he said.
Jesus had turned the water to wine.
This was the first of Jesus' many miracles.
Jesus was and is truly the Son of God.
                John 2:1-11

As Jesus walked along one day,
    a man came to Him.
The man's skin was spotted and blotchy.
Some of his fingers and toes were missing.
A terrible disease, leprosy, was killing him.
"Please, Jesus," said the man.
"I believe You are Christ the Lord.
I believe in God.
Please make me clean again.
Take away this terrible disease."
Jesus felt sorry for the man.
"You have faith in Me and My Father.
You shall be clean.
From this moment on your disease is gone."
Just as Jesus said, the man was made clean.
He ran off to tell everyone
    about the miracle that had happened.

Everywhere people came to Jesus.
They begged for His help.
Jesus never turned anyone away.
        Matthew 8:2-4, Mark 1:40-45, Luke 5:12-15

Once Jesus and His disciples were in a boat
    when a storm came up.
Jesus was asleep in the back of the boat.
The disciples were frightened
    and called for His help.
Jesus woke up and spoke
    to the wind and the waves.
"Peace! Be still!" He said.
The storm stopped.
The waters calmed.
The disciples were amazed.
"What kind of a man is this," they asked,
    "that even the wind and the sea obey Him?"
        Matthew 8:23-27, Mark 4:35-41, Luke 8:22-25

One day Jairus, a rich man, came to Jesus.
"My daughter is dying," he cried.
"She is only 12 years old.
You can make her well."
Jesus rested His hand on the man's shoulder.
"Take Me to her," He said.
Quickly Jairus led Jesus to his house.
But the girl had died.
Jesus entered the house.
The girl lay on a bed.
Jesus took the girl's hand in His own.
"Arise," He said softly.
Immediately the girl sat up.
It was as though she had never been ill.
"It's a miracle!" someone whispered.
"We have seen a great miracle!"
> *Matthew 9:18-19, 23-26, Mark 5:22-24, 35-43,*
> *Luke 8:40-41 49-56*

News of Jesus' miracles traveled everywhere.
Some said, "Only the Son of God
   could do these wonderful things."
Still there were others who said,
   "He is a magician," or "He is a devil's servant."
> *Matthew 12:23-24, Mark 3:22, Luke 11:14-15*

One day Jesus and His disciples
    crossed a wide sea.
On the shore waited five thousand people.
They had come to hear Jesus.
Jesus was happy to talk with the people.
All day He told them about God.
They listened to every word.
But they also became very hungry.
"Have we no food for these people?" asked Jesus.
His disciples shook their heads.
"We have no food," they said.
"Only one boy has food,"
    said the disciple Andrew.
"But he only has five loaves of bread
    and two fish."
The disciples smiled.
Five loaves of bread and two fish
    to feed five thousand people?
"It is enough," said Jesus.
He prayed to God the Father.
Then He told His disciples
    to begin feeding the people.
The disciples obeyed.
They took pieces of the bread and the fish.
The basket holding the food stayed full.
Again and again the disciples returned
    for bread and fish.
The people sat on the grass and ate.
Everyone had plenty of food.
Then the disciples picked up the crumbs.
There were 12 baskets of food left over!
It was another miracle!
    Matthew 14:13-21, Mark 6:32-44,
    Luke 9:11-17, John 6:1-14

One night Jesus walked alone beside the sea.
Big black clouds hid the moon.
Thunder rolled across the sky.
Wild waves slapped against the shore.
Jesus looked across the water.
His disciples were in a boat.
Angry waves pounded the ship.
The ship began to sink.
Quickly Jesus walked out on the water.
"Do not be afraid," Jesus told His helpers.
"Lord, if it's really You,
    tell me to come to You on the water,"
    said Peter.
"All right, come, Peter," Jesus answered.
"Walk with me."
Slowly Peter stepped out of the boat.
He walked across the water toward Jesus.
Suddenly Peter stopped.
"This must be a dream!" he shouted.
"I cannot walk on water."
Peter slipped into the waves.
"Help me, Jesus!" he begged.
Jesus stepped forward and took Peter's hand.
"Oh, Peter, you have such little faith!"
Peter nodded.
Yes, he had forgotten,
    but Jesus had saved him.
        Matthew 14:22-33, Mark 6:45-51, John 6:15-21

Everywhere people listened to Jesus.
Everywhere people watched the Lord.
But one could not. He was blind.
One day this blind man stepped forward.
"Lord, be kind to me," he said.
People pushed the blind man away.
They wanted to be closer to Jesus.
"Be kind to me, Lord," the blind man said louder.
Again the people pushed and shoved.
The blind man stumbled.
Jesus took his hand and held him.
"What is it you want?" Jesus asked.
"O Lord, please let me see."
Jesus smiled. "Your faith in God and in Me
     will let you see," he said.
Suddenly the man laughed.
He spun around, looking at everyone nearby.
"I can see!" he shouted.
"You are truly the Son of God."
        Mark 10:46-52, Luke 18:35-43

Jesus performed many, many more miracles.
He raised people from the dead.
Lazarus, His good friend,
     was dead and buried in a tomb.
But Jesus called his name,
        and Lazarus came out of the tomb alive.
        John 11:1-44

JESUS DIES

*J*esus had taught and healed
and performed wonderful miracles
for nearly three years.
His time here on earth
was almost finished.

Jesus led His disciples into the city of Jerusalem.
He rode on the back of a young donkey.
The people of the great city knew He was coming
and ran to meet Jesus.
"Welcome, Jesus!" the men shouted.
"Bless us, Jesus!" the women called.
"We love You, Jesus!" the children cheered.
People spread their cloaks on the ground.
People cut leaves from palm trees
and spread them on the ground.
They wanted Jesus to have a grand path
into their city.
"Who is this Jesus?" asked a stranger to the city.
"He is the Son of God!" one man answered.
"He is our Savior!" shouted another.
"He is our Teacher!" yelled a third man.
The people of Jerusalem cheered.
"We love You, Jesus."
Matthew 21:1-11, Mark 11:1-10,
Luke 19:29-40, John 12:12-15

Jesus was eager to visit the temple.
He wanted to pray in God's house.
He remembered when He was just a little boy,
what a fine and holy place the temple was!
But the temple was no longer the same.
It was dirty and noisy.
Men were selling goats and sheep.
They were counting money.
They were eating and drinking.

Jesus was angry at what He found in the temple.
"This should be a place for prayer!" He shouted.
"This is God's house,
    but it has become an evil place.
No one is praying here."
Jesus pushed over tables.
He pushed over chairs.
"Take your animals out of God's house," Jesus said.
"This is a place for people to pray and worship God."
The men ran from the temple.
They took their money and their goods.

"Now bring Me the people who are sick," said Jesus.
"Bring Me the people who cannot see and cannot walk."
The disciples of Jesus obeyed.
When the sick and blind and lame were brought in,
    Jesus prayed.
All who were there were cured.
        Matthew 21:12-14, Mark 11:15-17, Luke 19:45

Jesus continued to teach the people about God.
But the high officials of the temple in Jerusalem
        didn't like Jesus.
They feared His power.
They feared the people would follow Jesus
        and not them.
The evil men wanted to get rid of Jesus.
"The people love Him," the men said.
"They will do anything He asks.
He has too much power.
He must die!
Maybe we can get one of His disciples to help us."
Carefully the temple leaders made an evil plan.
        Matthew 26:3-5, Mark 14:1-2,
        Luke 22:2, John 11:47-53

A great holiday approached
    while Jesus was in Jerusalem.
This holiday was called the Passover.
"Let us have supper together,"
    Jesus told His disciples.
"Where shall we eat this supper?" asked Peter.
"We shall do as You wish," said John.
"Go to the gates of the city," said Jesus.
"You will find a man there carrying
    a pitcher of water.
Follow this man to his master's house.
Talk to the master of the house.
He will give us a room for our supper."
Peter and John did as Jesus said.
They found the man with the pitcher.
They followed him home and talked
    with the owner of the house.
"All friends of Jesus will be welcome here,"
    said the householder.
"I shall have everything ready."
Once again Peter and John were amazed.
Everything was always just as Jesus
    said it would be.
        Matthew 26:17-19, Mark 14:12-16, Luke 22:7-13

In Bible times people's feet would get very dusty
    from walking in sandals along unpaved roads.
Servants would usually wash the feet
    of guests at a supper.
But at this supper Jesus, the Master,
    washed the feet of His disciples.
"You call Me Lord," Jesus said, "and I am.
If I, then, have washed your feet,
    you also should humbly serve one another.
I have set you an example.
Do this, and you will be happy."
        John 13:1-17

"You have been My helpers for a long time,"
    Jesus said.
"But now one of you has turned against Me."
The disciples looked surprised.
Surely Jesus had made a mistake.
Not one of them would turn against Him.
But never before had Jesus made a mistake.
"Is it I, Lord?" Peter asked.
"Is it I, Lord?" Thomas asked.
"Is it I, Lord?" James asked.
Each disciple asked the same question.
Jesus said nothing.
One disciple lowered his head.
He hoped Jesus did not know that he was the one.
"Is it I, Lord?" Judas asked.
"You have said it," Jesus answered.
"Do quickly what you plan to do."
Judas left the room
    and went out into the night.
    Matthew 26:20-25, Mark 14:17-21,
    Luke 22:21-23, John 13:18-30

While they were eating, Jesus took some bread.
He spoke a blessing and then broke it into pieces.
"Take and eat it," He said to the disciples.
"This is My body."
Then He took a cup of wine.
After giving thanks, He gave it to them.
"Drink from it, all of you," He said.
"This is My blood,
      poured out for the forgiveness of sins.
I will soon be leaving you.
What you eat and drink here
      will remind you of Me after I am gone.
Do this to remember Me."
      Matthew 26:26-29, Mark 14:22-25,
      Luke 22:17-20, 1 Corinthians 11:23-26

The disciples ate the bread.
They drank from the cup.
But where was Jesus going? they wondered.
Jesus knew the question they were thinking.
"I will soon be going to the Father," He said.
"But God will not leave you without comfort.
He will send the Holy Spirit to be your Helper.
But will you come with Me now?"
They sang a hymn together,
      and then Jesus led them out.
Out into the night the twelve men walked.
Candlelight flickered in the dark city.
A light breeze stirred through the trees.
Jesus led the disciples
      through the streets of Jerusalem.
They walked out the city gates.

"Peter," Jesus said sadly,
"Before the rooster crows in the morning,
    you will three times deny that you know Me."
"No," said Peter, "Never!
I would die for You."
Jesus didn't argue.

Finally they came to a big garden.
It was called Gethsemane.
"Stay here," Jesus told Peter, James, and John.
"Watch and pray.
I am going over there to pray."
Jesus slowly walked further into the garden alone.
He was sad.
He fell to His knees.
"I love You, God," He prayed.
"I have lived for You and I will die,
    if it is Your will.
Stay with Me.
I need the strength You give."
Jesus returned to His disciples.
They lay on the ground.
"Why are you sleeping?" He asked.
"Will you come now and pray with Me?"
But the disciples moaned.
They were tired and wanted to sleep.
Jesus went back to pray alone.
For a long time Jesus prayed.
Finally God sent an angel to strengthen Him.
Soon Jesus knew He could face any danger.
God had given Jesus courage.

Lights appeared in the distance.
Like tiny fireflies they flickered.
Closer they came, and closer.
Voices shouted.
The enemies of Jesus had come.
Many of them were soldiers with swords.
The disciples of Jesus were frightened.
They jumped to their feet.
"What should we do?" asked John.
"There are too many to fight," Peter said.
"Let's run away and hide," said James.
Jesus stepped forward.
"Do not be afraid," He said.
"It's God's will that this should happen to Me.
God's prophets wrote about it long ago
    in the Bible."
The crowd came close.
A man walked up to Jesus.
It was Judas. He kissed Jesus to identify Him.
He had helped the enemies of Jesus for money.
"I am sorry for you, Judas," said Jesus sadly.

Quickly the crowd surrounded Jesus
    and His disciples.
"Leave Jesus alone," Peter shouted.
He cut off the ear of a man with his sword.
"Stay away from Jesus!"
"Put your sword down," said Jesus.
"It's against the laws of God to kill."
Jesus touched the man Peter had hurt.
Instantly the man's ear was healed.
The disciples did not know what to do.
They were confused and afraid,
    so they ran away and hid.
The crowd led Jesus out of the garden.
They took Him back to Jerusalem.

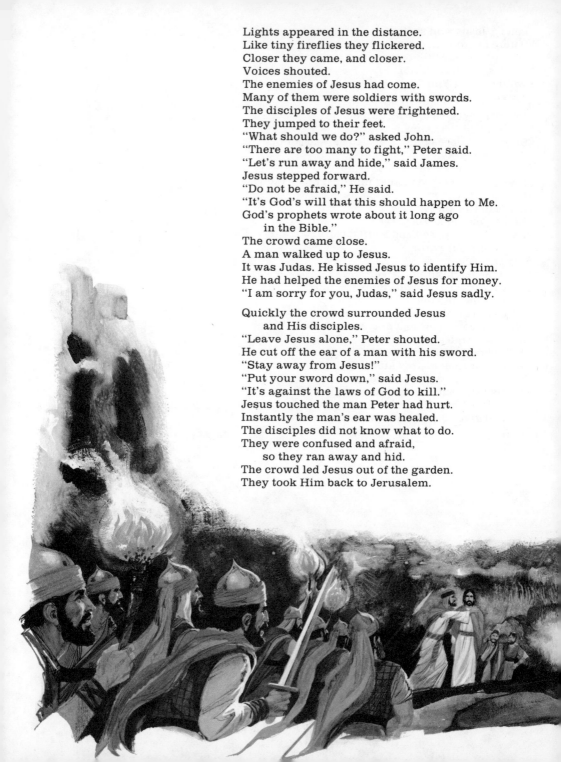

Jesus was taken before a group of religious leaders
    to answer charges brought against Him.
But they couldn't agree
    on why they should condemn Him.
Jesus said nothing.
Finally the high priest had an idea.
He turned to Jesus and solemnly said:
"Swear to me by the living God
    whether you are the Christ, the Son of God."
Now Jesus could no longer remain silent.
"You've said it; yes, I am," He replied.
In mock dismay the high priest tore his clothes.
"He has spoken against God!" he cried.
"What do you think?"
"He must die!" they answered.

While this was going on, Peter was warming himself
    by a fire in the courtyard.
Suddenly, a woman pointed her finger at Peter.
"You were with Jesus!" she said.
"No," Peter answered, his voice trembling.
"Weren't you His helper?" another asked Peter.
"No, no," Peter answered.
"I do not know Him."
Again someone said, "You were with
    the Man called Jesus."
"No, No, No," said Peter.
"I don't know what you're talking about."
Suddenly the rooster crowed
    in the early morning dawn.
Peter remembered that Jesus had said he would
    three times deny knowing Him.
Peter ran away.
He was ashamed and cried bitterly.

Meanwhile in a dark and lonely place
    Judas hanged himself.
    Matthew 26:30—27:10, Mark 14:26-72,
    Luke 22:31-71, John 13:31—14:31; 18:1-27

The crowd brought Jesus to Pilate,
　　the Roman governor.
"What has He done wrong?" Pilate asked.

What could Jesus have done so wrong?
Was it wrong to tell people
　　to love God and their neighbor?
Was it wrong to heal the sick?
Was it wrong to make the blind see?
Were these things wrong?

"Why have you brought this Man to me?"
　　Pilate asked the crowd.
"He says He is the Son of God,"
　　the temple leaders shouted.
"He calls Himself the Christ."
Pilate shook his head.
"This Man has done nothing wrong.
"But I will send Him to Herod.
Maybe he will find something wrong with Jesus."

Jesus was taken to Herod's house.
Herod mocked Jesus, then sent Him back to Pilate.

"Jesus has done nothing wrong," Pilate said again.
"I must let Him go."
"No!" the crowd shouted.
"He must die!
Let us have Him!"
Pilate was frightened.
He had never seen people so angry.
They were loud and shouting.
Finally, Pilate shook his head.
"Since it is your Passover,
　　I will free one prisoner.
Which will it be,
　　the criminal Barabbas or Jesus?"
"Give us Barabbas," the crowd shouted.
"Kill Jesus!"
Pilate washed his hands
　　and said it was their decision, not his.
He wanted no part in it.

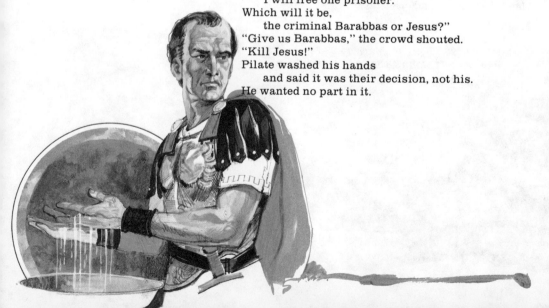

The soldiers and angry people took Jesus.
First they beat Him.
And Jesus bled.
"Jesus says He is a king!" one soldier shouted.
"A king should have a crown."
The soldiers made a crown from sharp thorns.
They put it on His head.
And Jesus bled.
"A king should be strong!" another soldier shouted.
"Let us see how strong He is."
The people hit Jesus and pushed Him.
And Jesus bled.
"A king should walk through His kingdom,"
    shouted a man.
"We will let Jesus walk among His people."
The soldiers gave Jesus a big wooden beam
    to carry on His shoulders.
And Jesus bled.
Matthew 27:11-31, Mark 15:1-20,
Luke 23:1-25, John 18:28—19:16

Slowly Jesus walked
    through the streets of Jerusalem.
The cross was heavy.
Jesus stumbled.
The people laughed.
On Jesus walked, and on and on.
Finally He came to a hill called Golgotha.
The soldiers made Jesus walk up the hill.
Then they nailed Jesus to the cross He had carried.
They tied Him to the beam, then drove nails
    through His hands and feet.
The soldiers raised Him up.

Sadly Jesus looked down at the people.
Although He was suffering, He still loved them.
They didn't realize He was dying for them.
"Forgive them, Father," Jesus prayed.
"They do not know what they are doing."
Slowly the minutes slipped by.
The soldiers gambled for His cloak.
Jesus asked John to care for His mother, Mary.
Jesus forgave one of the thieves beside Him,
    who repented of His sins
    and asked for forgiveness.
Jesus promised the thief that that very day
    he would be in heaven with Him.
One hour passed.
Then two.
Then three.
The bright golden sun became dark.
It was almost as though it couldn't bear
    to look at the suffering Jesus.
Finally Jesus asked for water.
After they gave Him some,
    He cried out, "It is finished!"
"Father," He said again, "I am coming to You."
Then Jesus died.

Suddenly the earth shook.
Thunder rolled through the air.
The centurian who was in charge said,
    "Truly this man was the Son of God."

A man named Joseph of Arimathea,
        who had secretly been a friend of Jesus,
        asked Pilate for permission to bury the body.
Pilate let him.
Gently he and Nicodemus (the secret friend
        who long ago had come to Jesus by night),
        together with some brave women,
        took Jesus' body down from the cross.
"He was our Savior," said John,
        the only disciple who did not run and hide.
"He was the Son of God," said Mary Magdalene,
        one of Jesus' followers.
"We shall wrap Him in clean cloth
        and put spices on Him," said Nicodemus.
"And we will put Him in my tomb,"
        said Joseph of Arimathea.
The friends of Jesus did these things.
Then they rolled a giant stone to block
        the entrance to the tomb.
"No one can bother Him now," they said.
They went away sad and brokenhearted.
    Matthew 27:32-61, Mark 15:21-47,
    Luke 23:26-56, John 19:17-42

JESUS LIVES!

On the morning of the third day
Mary Magdalene, Mary the mother of James,
and Salome came to the tomb
with spices to put on Jesus' body.
But they could not believe what they saw.
The stone had been moved!
The tomb was empty!
Jesus was gone!

Suddenly an angel appeared.
His face was as bright as lightning.
His clothing was as white as snow.
"Do not be afraid," he said.
"Jesus has risen from the dead.
Find His disciples.
Tell them Jesus has gone to Galilee.
He will see them there."

Away the friends of Jesus ran.
They went to find the disciples.
They went to share the good news.
"Jesus is alive!" they sang out in joy.
"He is the resurrected Lord!"
"Jesus is alive!"
"Jesus is alive!"
The news became a happy song
    to people everywhere.
"But how can it be?" some people still asked.
"Jesus died on the cross.
A man cannot die and bring himself
    back to life."
"Jesus can!" His believers shouted.
"He is not just a man.
He is the Son of God.
He is our Savior.
He is our resurrected Lord."

The disciples traveled to Galilee.
They waited for Jesus to come.
"Friends," He said, "you have been good workers.
But there is more you must do."
The disciples listened closely.
They wanted to hear every word Jesus said.
"You must travel everywhere," Jesus continued.
"Tell all people to believe in Me
    as their Savior.
Baptize them in the name of the Father
    and of the Son and of the Holy Spirit.
Tell them to follow God's rules.
Those who believe and are baptized
    will go to heaven.
I must return to My heavenly Father,
    but I will be with you all the time
    with My love and My power."

The disciples went back to Jerusalem.
Jesus appeared to them again
    and led them out of the city
    to the Mount of Olives.
Jesus blessed His disciples.
Slowly His body rose into the sky.
Higher He ascended, and higher.
Finally He was out of sight.
"Jesus is gone," one disciple said.
Peter smiled.
"No," he said.
"He is with us.
He is with everyone who believes
    in Him and His teachings."
    Matthew 28:1-10, 16-20, Mark 16:1-20,
    Luke 24:1-11, 33-53, John 20:1—21:14, Acts 1:1-11

This is the wonderful story of Jesus,
    our Savior and Lord!